Dog

By Barney Saltzberg

Hooked On Phonics®

ISBN 1-887942-30-0

"What is in the cup?
It looks a lot like a dog."

"It looks a lot like a bug, too!"
"What is it? A dog? A bug?"

"I can wag like a dog.
But I can zip like a bug!
I am a Dog Bug."

"Look! Lots and lots of Dog Bugs!"

"2 Dog Bugs can zip and dip."

"3 Dog Bugs can zip, dip, and hop."

"Look what 10 Dog Bugs can do!"